Learn|ng Short-take™

CATHERINE MATTISKE

Understanding Relationship Selling

How to Build Customer's Rapport,
Respect & Trust

TPC - The Performance Company Pty Ltd
PO Box 639
Rozelle NSW 2039
Sydney, Australia

ACN 077 455 273
email: info@tpc.net.au
Website: www.tpc.net.au

National Library of Australia
Cataloguing-in-Publication data

Mattiske, Catherine
Understanding Relationship Selling: How to Build Customer's Rapport, Respect & Trust

ISBN 978-1-921547-19-5

1. Occupational training   2. Learning   I. Title

370.113

Printed in USA

Distributed by TPC - The Performance Company - www.tpc.net.au
For further information contact TPC - The Performance Company, Sydney Australia on +61 9555 1953 or TPC - The Performance Company, California on +1 818-227-5052, or email info@tpc.net.au

hello.

Welcome to the TPC Learning Short-take™ process!

This Learning Short-take™ is a bite sized learning package that aims to improve your skills and provide you with an opportunity for personal and professional development to achieve success in your role.

**This Learning Short-take™ combines self study with workplace activities in a unique learning system to keep you motivated and energized.
So let's get started!**

Step 1:
What's inside?

- Learning Short-take™ Participant Guide. This section contains all of the learning content and will guide you through the learning process.
- Learning Activities. You will be prompted to complete these as you read through the Participant Guide.
- Learning Journal. This is a summary of your key learnings. Update it when prompted.
- Skill Development Action Plan. Learning is about taking action. This is your action plan where you'll plan how you will implement your learning.

Step 2:
Complete the Learning Short-take™

- Learning Short-takes™ are best completed in a quiet environment that is free of distractions.
- Schedule time in your calendar to complete the Learning Short-take™ and prioritize this time as an investment in your own professional development.
- Depending on the title, most participants complete the Learning Short-take™ from 90 minutes to 2.5 hours.

Step 3:
Meet with your Manager/Coach

- Schedule a 30 minute meeting with your Manager or Coach.
- At this meeting share your completed Activities, Learning Journal and Skill Development Action Plan.
- Most importantly, discuss and agree on how you will implement your learning in your role.

Welcome

Understanding Relationship Selling
How to Build Customer's Rapport, Respect & Trust

This Learning Short-take™ aims to provide you with specific skill development in relationship selling.

The focus of this Learning Short-take™ is to help you understand the value of building relationships with your customers to facilitate repeat business and active referrals.

You will be undertaking a process of self-assessment, reflection and skill review, and be able to use this awareness as a solid base for ongoing personal development and success in your role.

Now let's get started!

"The single most important thing to remember about any enterprise is that there are no results inside its walls. The result of a business is a satisfied customer."

Peter Drucker

Section 1

Participant Guide

Start here →

What's in this Participant Guide

"Customers don't
expect you to be perfect.
They do expect you to
fix things when they
go wrong."

Donald Porter, British Airways

Table of Contents

How to Complete your Learning Short-take™

1. Reflect on your skills and Abilities in managing sales relationships, and how well you use these skills to achieve success in your role.

2. Complete the Initial Skills Assessment.

3. Highlight specific skill areas that you believe you could develop more. Add these to the Learning Journal. Add to your Learning Journal as you go.

4. When you have completed this Learning Short-take™ meet with your Manager/Coach. In this meeting, you will jointly establish a personal Skill Development Action Plan.

5. Subject to your coach's final review and assessment, you will either sign off the module, or undertake further skill development as appropriate.

"Coming together is a beginning. Keeping together is progress. Working together is success."

Henry Ford

Activity Checklist

During this Learning Short-take™ you will be prompted to complete the following activities:

"Being on par in terms of price and quality only gets you into the game. Service wins the game."

Tony Alessandra

Learning Objectives

- Define relationship selling

- Explain the difference between traditional selling and relationship selling

- State key differences between product-based selling and needs-based selling

- Explain the importance of trust in relationship selling

- Explain the principles of relationship selling

- Describe how to maintain a relationship even when the answer is 'no'

- Identify the steps in the relationship selling process

- Create a Skill Development Action Plan

"Quality in a service or product is not what you put into it. It is what the client or customer gets out of it."

Peter Drucker

Let's Get Started

Relationships are key to sales success. Many professional sales people have strong selling skills yet continue to lose business to competitors due to failure to establish genuine relationships with their customers. They may have the right product at the right price, but they will lose to the competitor with the right relationship.

A truly competent sales person establishes a relationship in which he or she provides a much needed and appreciated service to customers - a trusted professional who provides guidance in solving business problems.

This Learning Short-take™ combines self-study with workplace activities to develop skills in relationship selling. Participants will compare traditional selling techniques with more modern sales processes based on the development of trust, rapport and empathy.

Participants will evaluate their own approach to selling, and develop new and innovative strategies to foster key relationships, understand customer needs, and provide appropriate sales solutions.

tpc

Getting Started

Part 1

What is Relationship Selling

In selling there is one simple truth - most of the business you do is based on the relationships that you have with your customers, and your best customers are the ones with whom you have the best relationships. Relationship selling is simple. If you want your customers to come back they have to like you, respect you and trust you. Relationship selling is about increasing understanding of customer needs, providing meaningful solutions to customer problems, and fulfilling sales commitments. The objective is to build sales relationships that grow and continue to create value long after the first sale, boosting long term sales and profitability.

"85 percent of the happiness and success you enjoy in life will be determined by the quality of relationships with others."

Brian Tracy

Relationship selling is based on the premise that the best source of new business is existing customers, and referrals from existing customers.

This approach requires a long term commitment to providing ongoing customer satisfaction, rather than a short term focus on making sales.

While relationship selling may take longer to produce a result, the organization will be rewarded with high levels of repeat business, new business, and referrals from satisfied customers.

Complete Activity # 1
Initial Skills Assessment

Activity 1: Initial Skills Assessment

Understanding how to develop effective customer relationships is critical to improving sales success. This assessment covers the key skills for building customer relationships in order to sustain and develop your business.

Rate yourself on each of the techniques.

7   is competent and confident, little need for improvement

4   is average, needs improvement

1   is uncomfortable, major need for improvement

- Note specific areas of improvement related to each that you would like to develop. Be sure to include your reasons for your rating in each skill.
- As part of starting to think about a personal development plan, identify two or three things you could do to improve your skills in this area and write them in the space provided.

I...	Rating	Reasoning
invest the majority of my selling time in building trust and rapport with my customers.	1 2 3 4 5 6 7	
tell my customers the truth. If my product isn't right for them I let them know.	1 2 3 4 5 6 7	
keep my promises and deliver more than is expected.	1 2 3 4 5 6 7	
understand my customers and really get to know their business and their customers.	1 2 3 4 5 6 7	
am professional, ethical and considerate in my interactions with customers.	1 2 3 4 5 6 7	

Activity 1: Continued

I...	Rating	Reasoning
understand that repeat business and referrals from my customers is critical to business longevity.	1 2 3 4 5 6 7	
value customer relationships over making a quick sale.	1 2 3 4 5 6 7	
use thorough questioning techniques to understand the unique buying motivations of my customers.	1 2 3 4 5 6 7	
actively listen to what my customers are telling me and demonstrate that I have understood their needs.	1 2 3 4 5 6 7	
spend little time on closing sales because I build rapport and identify needs very effectively.	1 2 3 4 5 6 7	
aim to achieve a win-win result in every customer transaction.	1 2 3 4 5 6 7	
make follow-up contact as often as necessary with my customers to confirm that they are satisfied.	1 2 3 4 5 6 7	
keep my word and partner with customers to resolve problems even when unexpected issues come up.	1 2 3 4 5 6 7	

Personal development plan ideas:

1

2

Now update your Learning Journal (page 59)

Traditional versus Modern Approaches to Selling

"Your professionalism is defined not by the business you are in, but by the way you are in business."

Tony Alessandra

Traditional Approaches to Selling

Influence Selling

Much of the development of selling skills and conventional sales training is attributed to the American writer, speaker and businessman Dale Carnegie (1888 - 1955). Carnegie's 1937 self-help book 'How to Win Friends and Influence People' - a work on human motivation, relationships and influence, was as major source of the theory which underpins traditional selling. Based on Carnegie's work, traditional selling methods encourage sales people to use knowledge about the customer, gain their trust, and lead them in a certain direction.

The primary focus is on 'influencing' the customer to take action in the direction which favours the salesperson, whether this is in the genuine best interest of the customer or not.

14

While Carnegie and others who have developed his early ideas, provide a good framework for understanding other people's needs and motives in the sales process, the matters of ethics, honesty and integrity are omitted. Used unethically, this process amounts to customer manipulation and is not sustainable for long term sales success.

Funnel Selling

The majority of salespeople have been trained in "funnel selling" at some point in their sales career. Funnel selling is based on the premise that the more cold calls you make, the more sales you make at the end of the funnel. While this method of selling can be successful purely on a volume basis, it doesn't consider the selling environment inside the funnel, or how you take the customer from the first appointment through the sales cycle to the close.

The disadvantage of this approach is that the energies of the salesperson are not being used synergistically, that is, they expend energy on a high volume of individual calls instead of forming the relationships needed to sustain repeat business.

> "Customers do not buy products.
> They buy solutions to a problem."
>
> Jack Collis

Product Selling

Traditional approaches to selling also focus heavily on 'product' and selling the product offering, ie. how the product or service is described and promoted to the customer in advertising and promotional material. Typically this will include feature and benefit statements, developed by the seller and aimed at the target market.

While benefit selling is a critical part of the sales process, benefit statements are largely formulated from the seller's perspective and not in response to individual customer needs. The disadvantage of this approach is failure to recognize the unique buying motives of the customer. It also limits competitive advantage in a saturated market where there is an oversupply of products with very similar if not identical features.

In this type of market it is critical to uncover real customer needs and partner with the customer to provide a genuine solution to their problem. Long term business survival is dependant on the development of a sustainable business relationship with opportunity for repeat business.

Modern Approaches to Selling

Consultative Selling

Consultative selling involves deeper questioning of the customer that extends beyond the product itself, and explores real customer needs.

Consultative selling seeks to uncover not just what the product will 'do' for the customer, but how it will make them 'feel', thereby tuning into their unique buying motivations. This leads to greater understanding of the customer's wider needs (particularly those affected by the product) and the questioning process itself results in greater trust, rapport and empathy between salesperson and customer (relationship selling). Consultative selling depends on the salespersons ability, experience and expertise to 'consult' with the buyer in developing a solution to their problem, becoming an expert in the customers business as well as their own.

Relationship Selling

Relationship selling is a way of conducting business that is flexible, cooperative and professional. When selling in the context of a healthy relationship, salespeople are able to operate in an ethical, considerate and helpful manner. In relationship selling the salesperson becomes a form of support for the customer, providing products and services that they come to depend on, creating a steady stream of sales for the business. Selling through true collaboration and partnership creates a sustainable platform for supplier and customer to work together, building relationships that take selling to new heights of sophistication and competitive advantage.

Essential components of the relationship selling model are:

- **Truth:** Customers expect that if your product or service isn't right for them, you'll let them know.
- **Reliability:** Customers want to know you'll be there when they need you, you'll keep your promises and you'll deliver more than is expected.
- **Understanding:** True understanding means listening to customer needs, getting to know their objectives, and figuring out what they want to accomplish.
- **Service:** What do you do to differentiate yourself? Do you give value-added service so customers will be willing to pay more?

Partnership Selling

Partnership Selling is an extension of Relationship Selling where customers see the salesperson and the selling organization as a true partner in their business. At this point the customer and salesperson enjoy a genuine friendship and ease of doing business. While these customers keep the opportunity for ongoing sales strong, it is at this point that the salesperson can re-enter the sales funnel, reinforcing the customer base for future success.

"The very best salespeople are 'relationship experts'. They focus all of their attention on the relationship before they begin talking about their products or services."

Brian Tracy

Complete Activity # 2
Terms & Definitions Match

Activity 2: Terms & Definitions Match

Draw a line to match the project management term with it's correct definition.

Product Selling

Consultative Selling

Relationship Selling

Funnel Selling

Partnership Selling

Influence Selling

Persuading the customer to take action in a direction which favours the salesperson, whether this is in the genuine best interest of the customer or not. Used unethically this type of selling amounts to customer manipulation and is not sustainable for long term sales success.

Based on the premise that the more cold calls you make the more sales you make. While this method of selling can be successful purely on a volume basis, it doesn't consider the selling environment or the relationships needed to facilitate repeat business.

Typically this involves features and benefits selling and is largely formulated from the seller's perspective and not in response to individual customer needs. The disadvantage of this approach is failure to recognize the unique buying motives of the customer. It also limits competitive advantage in a saturated market where there is an oversupply of products with similar features.

Involves deeper questioning of the customer that extends beyond the product itself, and explores real customer needs. Seeks to uncover not just what the product will 'do' for the customer, but how it will make them 'feel', thereby tuning into their unique buying motivations.

The salesperson becomes a form of support for the customer, providing products and services that they come to depend on. Based on the fundamentals of truth, reliability, understanding and service.

An extension of relationship selling where customers see the salesperson and the selling organization as a true partner in their business. At this point the customer and salesperson enjoy a genuine friendship and ease of doing business.

Activity # 2 - Check your Answers

Terms	Definitions
Influence Selling	Persuading the customer to take action in a direction which favours the salesperson, whether this is in the genuine best interest of the customer or not. Used unethically this type of selling amounts to customer manipulation and is not sustainable for long term sales success.
Funnel Selling	Based on the premise that the more cold calls you make the more sales you make. While this method of selling can be successful purely on a volume basis, it doesn't consider the selling environment or the relationships needed to facilitate repeat business.
Product Selling	Typically this involves features and benefits selling and is largely formulated from the seller's perspective and not in response to individual customer needs. The disadvantage of this approach is failure to recognize the unique buying motives of the customer. It also limits competitive advantage in a saturated market where there is an oversupply of products with similar features.
Consultative Selling	Involves deeper questioning of the customer that extends beyond the product itself, and explores real customer needs. Seeks to uncover not just what the product will 'do' for the customer, but how it will make them 'feel', thereby tuning into their unique buying motivations.
Relationship Selling	The salesperson becomes a form of support for the customer, providing products and services that they come to depend on. Based on the fundamentals of truth, reliability, understanding and service.
Partnership Selling	An extension of relationship selling where customers see the salesperson and the selling organization as a true partner in their business. At this point the customer and salesperson enjoy a genuine friendship and ease of doing business.

Now update your Learning Journal (page 59)

Evolution of Selling

Part 2

Evolution of the Selling Function

Today, more is demanded from the selling process than ever before. The modern customer is more sophisticated and requires higher levels of customer service and support. They want to work with and buy from people that they trust, who understand their unique needs and wants. This is particularly important in slow economic times when customers make buying decisions very carefully.

The analysis below outlines the development of the sales function in recent years, highlighting what customers require from the selling function, and the progression of a relationship between supplier and customer.

1. Pure Transaction: Basic early selling - standard commodity products, price and reliability - there is little to build on, business may be spasmodic, hand-to-mouth and unpredictable.

2. Relationship and Trust: Continuity, consistency, sustainability, and some understanding of the customer's real issues are seen to have value by both selling and buying organization; intangibles begin to be regarded as relevant benefits.

4. Partnership: Activities of the buying and selling organization become almost seamless; the supplier is virtually part of the customer's organization and treated as such; there is a level of anticipation, innovation and integrated support that is very difficult to un-pick, even if it were in the customer's interests to do so. This is the pinnacle of relationship selling.

3. Management and Information: A longer-term supply arrangement is seen as an advantage by seller and buyer, because it brings extra intangible benefits of co-operation and support other areas of the customer's business – improving the customer's own competitive strengths and operating efficiencies.

The Changing Face of Selling - A Summary

Traditional Selling	Modern Selling
standard product	customized, flexible, tailored product and service
seller has product knowledge	seller has strategic knowledge of customer's market-place and knows all implications and opportunities resulting from product/service supply relating to customer's market-place
value is represented and judged according to selling price	value is assessed according to the cost to the customer, plus non-financial implications with respect to CSR (corporate social responsibility), environment, ethics, and corporate culture
benefits of supply extend to products and services only	benefits of supply extend way beyond products and services, to relationship, continuity, and any assistance that the selling organization can provide to the customer.
seller knows the customers needs	seller knows the needs of the customers' customers, partners and suppliers
strategic emphasis is on new business growth (ie, acquiring new customers)	strategic emphasis is on customer retention and increasing business to those customers (although new business is still sought)
the customer specifies and identifies product and service requirements	the selling organization is capable of specifying and identifying product and service requirements on behalf of the customer
the customer does not appreciate his/her organization's wider strategic implications and opportunities in relation to the seller's product or service.	the seller will help the customer to understand the wider strategic implications and opportunities in relation to the seller's product or service

"Do a little bit more than average and from that point on your progress multiplies itself out of all proportion to the effort put in."

Paul J. Meyer

Complete Activity # 3a
Recruitment Ad Campaign

Complete Activity # 3b
Recruitment Ad Campaign

Widgets Inc. is a manufacturer and distributor of widgets. Due to market acceptance of a new product range and an increasing customer base, Widgets Inc. is seeking to expand their sales force. Widgets Inc. is looking to recruit 100 new salespeople nationally to cope with the increased demand and volume of sales.

activity 3(a)

Imagine that you are in charge of drafting a recruitment ad on behalf of Widgets Inc.

In this exercise you are preparing a newspaper ad for the year **1970**.

Think about the skills and abilities of the salespeople that you are seeking to hire, and the various job tasks that they will perform.

Ensure that your ad covers key job competencies and responsibilities.

Develop the ad according to the format on the reverse side of this sheet.

1

Widgets Inc.
Salespeople Wanted!

Widgets Inc. is a manufacturer and distributor of widgets. Due to market acceptance of a new product range and an increasing customer base, Widgets Inc is seeking to expand their sales force. If you have the desire to 'sell' and have the following skills and experience, apply now!

Skills:

Experience:

Responsibilities:

Applications should be forwarded to: Recruitment Manager, Widgets Inc • 10 Widget Way, Widget Town USA

Now update your Learning Journal (page 59)

activity 3(b)

Now imagine that you are in charge of drafting a recruitment ad on behalf of Widgets Inc. in the year **2006**.

Think about the skills and abilities of the salespeople that you are seeking to hire, and the various job tasks that they will perform.

Ensure that your ad covers key job competencies and responsibilities.

Develop the ad according to the format on the reverse side of this sheet.

1

Widgets Inc.
Salespeople Wanted!

Widgets Inc. is a manufacturer and distributor of widgets. Due to market acceptance of a new product range and an increasing customer base, Widgets Inc is seeking to expand their sales force. If you have the desire to 'sell' and have the following skills and experience, apply now!

Skills:

Experience:

Responsibilities:

Applications should be forwarded to: Recruitment Manager, Widgets Inc • 10 Widget Way, Widget Town USA

Now update your Learning Journal (page 59)

Relationship Selling Model

Part 3

Inside the Sales Call

The Relationship Selling Model vs The Traditional Selling Model

The graph below shows the different aims and objectives of relationship selling and traditional selling during a sales call. Clearly the focus in the Relationship model is to establish an environment of trust and support, and uncover real customer needs. Once established the process of 'selling' and 'closing' is a matter of course as opposed to a time and energy consuming process. Conversely, in the Traditional model, so little time is invested in the relationship and uncovering customer needs, that the process of 'selling' and 'closing' becomes an energy and time exhausting practice.

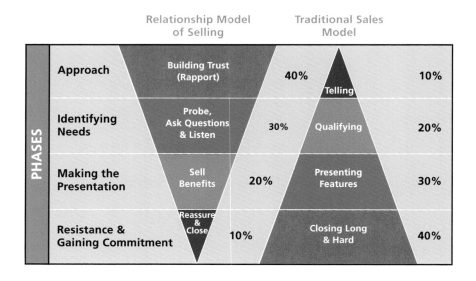

	Relationship Model of Selling		Traditional Sales Model	
Approach	Building Trust (Rapport)	40%	Telling	10%
Identifying Needs	Probe, Ask Questions & Listen	30%	Qualifying	20%
Making the Presentation	Sell Benefits	20%	Presenting Features	30%
Resistance & Gaining Commitment	Reassure & Close	10%	Closing Long & Hard	40%

PHASES

The Relationship Model

Step 1 - The Approach (40%)

The greatest investment of time is in 'approaching' the customer. The salesperson has one opportunity to get this right, and establishing a basis of trust and respect is critical to the ultimate success of the sale.

In order to do this well, the salesperson should introduce themselves, act genuinely and professionally, and create an environment in which the customer feels comfortable to talk about their problems and desires. When there is an environment of rapport and mutual respect, only then can the salesperson move to Step 2 to uncover real customer needs.

Step 2 - Identifying Needs (30%)

Again, a solid investment of time is required to complete this step effectively. The primary tool used at this stage of the process is questioning. Good questioning uncovers unique buying motivations, and also continues to build on the trust and rapport established in step 1. Open questions solicit the most comprehensive information because they provoke thinking and responses about customer facts and feelings in a non-threatening way. Active listening is also critical at this point, demonstrating to the customer that they have been heard and understood. Doing this step well, makes transition in the presentation stage a lot simpler.

Step 3 - Making the Presentation (20%)

At this point, the selling environment created in Steps 1 and 2 means that a much smaller amount of time and energy needs to be invested in selling benefits. The salesperson already has a refined understanding of customer needs, and now simply matches those needs to the unique benefits of the product or service in question.

The salesperson does not waste time presenting features and benefits that are of little or no use to the customer, because they have a thorough understanding of the customers individual buying motivations. They simply sell a solution to the customer's problem.

Step 4 - Gaining Commitment (10%)

By Step 4, reassuring the customer and closing the sale are almost a formality. At this stage, the customer has so much confidence in the salespersons ability to help them solve their problem, that they have virtually closed the sale themselves. The salesperson simply asks the customer to make a decision and take action on the product or service being offered.

The Traditional Model

Step 1 - Telling (10%)

In this process the salesperson invests little or no time establishing a relationship with the customer. Instead, the salesperson begins to 'tell' the customer about the particular product or service without 'asking' the customer anything about their needs. This results in an environment which is not based on mutual trust and respect and prevents the natural flow of conversation around customer buying motivations.

Step 2 - Qualifying (20%)

Again in this model the salesperson does not invest the required amount of time uncovering real customer needs. Failure to ask open and probing questions prevents the salesperson from understanding the customer's problem and therefore prevents them from assisting the customer to solve it. This lack of attention in the qualifying phase results in a presentation to the customer in Step 3 that is potentially unsuited to their needs and of little or no interest.

Step 3 - Presenting Features (30%)

Given the lack of time and energy invested in Steps 1 and 2 above, the sales process is about to get very busy and very complicated. Having failed to establish customer needs, the salesperson is forced to present every feature and benefit that the product or service has to offer, in the hope that at least one of these is important to the customer. This step takes a lot longer because the presentation cannot be targeted to the unique buying motivations of the customer.

Step 4 - Closing (40%)

As per Step 3 above, the salesperson is now lost in the process of meeting resistance, handling objections and trying to close the sale. Closing will be particularly difficult given that the salesperson has failed to qualify customer needs. This increases the number and intensity of objections and if handled poorly can lead to a full blown argument. Trying to get the customer to imagine owning or using the product or service at this point will be a long and exhausting process.

Given the complexity of products and services today...

"Customers are usually unable to make an accurate judgement on the details of what you are selling. Instead, they have to depend upon how they feel about you and your claims. For most customers today, the relationship comes first. It is more important than the product or service itself." Brian Tracy

Complete Activity # 4
Implementing the Relationship Model

Activity 4: Implementing the Relationship Model

What does your selling model currently look like? Identify your activities in each phase of the selling process and the percentage of time that you spend at each level.

Phase	What are you doing in this phase?	What % of time do you spend in this phase?
Approach	Building Trust ○ Telling ○	
Identifying Needs	Probing, Questioning, Listening ○ Qualifying ○	
Making the Presentation	Selling Benefits ○ Presenting Features ○	
Resistance & Gaining Commitment	Reassuring & Closing ○ Closing long and hard ○	

Complete the triangle according to your activities above.

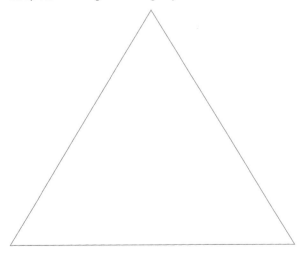

Please turn over to complete activity.

Activity 4: Continued

1 I could improve my "Approach" in Phase 1 by...

I could "Identify Needs" more effectively in Phase 2 by...
(NB. Be specific and include actual questions that you could use to stimulate conversation with your customers).

Now update your Learning Journal (page 59)

Relationship Selling Principles

Part 4

Principles of
Relationship Selling

It costs more than five times as much to attract a new customer as it does to keep an existing one. That in itself should help you understand the value of relationship selling.

"There is only one boss. The customer. And he can fire everybody in the company from the chairman on down, simply by spending his money somewhere else."

Sam Walton

In relationship selling you become a form of support for your customer. Your products and services become something they depend on, and the more you satisfy their needs the more they will respond to additional sales that you offer. You will also benefit from repeat business and referrals in competitive markets where there is little difference between products. Building an effective sales relationship is based on a number of inputs.

Trust

In any relationship, trust is a critical factor. Customers tend to do business with people they like and trust. This takes time to build, particularly for customers to accept that the salesperson will always have their best interests at heart.

Trust is established by letting your customers get to know you, and by you genuinely showing an interest in getting to know them and their business.

The better your product or service fits your customer's needs, the greater their trust in your ability to assist them, and the more sales you will have. When customers know you sincerely care about what they want and need, they will feel secure that they are making the right decision in buying from you.

Even if a customer does not have a need for your product or service, you can still build a trust relationship. By being honest and referring the customer to a more suitable resource, your good deed may be returned in the form of referral business.

"Honesty is the first chapter of the book of wisdom."

Thomas Jefferson

Keeping up Contact

A key part of relationship selling is maintaining regular contact. You should make follow-up contact with the customer as often as necessary to confirm that the customer is happy with the product or service deliverables.

Customer follow-up is always your responsibility even if well organized customer service arrangements exist for after sales care. Customers rightly hold salespeople responsible for what happens after the sale and good, conscientious follow-up will often be rewarded with referrals to other customers. Follow-up is also an important indicator of integrity and when you make a sale you are personally endorsing the product and the company. Ensuring that the customer satisfaction element is complete is an integral part of the sales function. If you neglect a customer who has trust in your integrity as a salesperson, that customer may finally be forced to turn to your competitors. It is important to make sure you not only develop a relationship, but establish regular channels of communication and contact.

Keeping your Word

Perhaps one of the most important ways
to develop customer relationships and
maintain trust is to keep your word.
From follow-up calls to delivering on
time, keeping your word can be a very
powerful sales tool.

Even when unexpected issues crop up and you are prevented from keeping
a promise, communicate with your customer immediately. Inquire whether
changes to commitments can be managed by the customer and what
you can do to actively lessen the inconvenience. By partnering with the
customer to resolve any problems you keep your trust level in tact and may
even strengthen it as a result.

Achieving Win-Win

Relationship selling has to end up as a win-win exchange. The
salesperson wants the customer to feel that they have got a fair deal,
and the customer (although they want a good price), does not want the
salesperson to go out of business. Many negotiables beyond price are on
the table, including goodwill and future sales opportunities. Relationship
selling is more successful when both parties consider the importance of
the relationship as well as whatever it is that they each want.

"The self image is they key to human personality and human behavior. Change the self image and you change the personality and the behavior."

Maxwell Maltz

Positioning yourself as a Professional

Great salespeople see themselves as advisors, helpers, problem solvers and friends to their customers. Yet perhaps the most important single determinant of whether or not someone buys from you is how the person thinks and feels about you. This is the very foundation of relationship selling is called 'positioning'. The position you have in the heart and mind of your customer is determined by the words that your customer uses when they describe you to others.

Furthermore, how your customers describe you is largely determined by how you define yourself. It is important to remember the first rule of self-image psychology: the person you see is the person you will be, and will determine how you behave on the outside. The best positioning you can have among your customers is that of a professional, an authority in your area of expertise. When you walk, talk and act like a professional; you set yourself apart from those who see themselves as salespeople.

Communication Excellence

(i) Ask open questions

One of the best ways to establish rapport with a customer is to ask questions that elicit information about their particular needs. The classic open questions begin with "who, what, when, where and how", and are useful because they promote responses about customer facts and feelings. (Use 'why'  questions sparingly as they force the customer to defend or justify their actions and prevent the development of trust and rapport). While you are asking questions, respond at appropriate times by linking key product or service benefits with the customers stated needs. The result is an interactive conversation where information is exchanged and both parties have an opportunity to expand their knowledge.

(ii) Listen more than you talk

Positive selling relationships are established when the salesperson gives their undivided attention to the customer. The ability to focus on the customer without interrupting or thinking about what you will say next is a rare skill. When you demonstrate that you can listen more than you talk, customers realize that you are genuinely interested in them and that you are trying to understand their unique needs and situation. The more they feel comfortable with you, the more they will tell you, and will soon realize that you are on their side. It is important to listen carefully and emphatically to demonstrate that you understand not just what has been said, but also what is being felt.

"Here is a simple but powerful rule - always give people more than what they expect to get."

Nelson Boswell

(iii) Interpret and use body language

Knowing how to interpret a customer's body language can give you much needed information about how comfortable they are with you, and how ready they are to make a purchase decision. Similarly, when you know how to use body language appropriately you can communicate your interest and concern for the customer without saying anything. This is helpful in establishing a trust relationship, and interacting as an ethical, considerate and helpful human being.

Complete Activity # 5
Positioning Yourself as a Professional

Activity 5: Positioning Yourself as a Professional

Identify your top three customers:

1. _____

2. _____

3. _____

For each of these customers, think about and record how you could implement the principles of relationship selling and establish yourself as a true professional. Be specific for each customer as they will have different needs and different expectations of you.

Customer	Strategies for building trust	Strategies for improving contact	Strategies for keeping my word
1.			
2.			
3.			

Activity 5: Continued

Customer	Strategies for achieving win/win	Strategies for improving professionalism	Strategies for improving communication
1.			
2.			
3.			

Now update your Learning Journal (page 59)

tpc ★

Relationship Builders
and Breakers

Part 5

Relationship Builders & Relationship Breakers

Relationship Builders	Relationship Breakers
• Treat customers like life-long partners	• Waiting for a problem to develop
• Become a solutions provider	• Focusing only on making the sale
• Deliver more service than you promise	• Over-promise and under-deliver
• Schedule regular service calls	• Wait for your customers to call you
• Develop open and honest communication	• Lie or make exaggerated claims
• Use the 'we can' approach	• Use the "us versus them" approach
• Take responsibility for mistakes made	• Blame somebody else
• Be an ally for the customers' business	• Knock a competitor
	• Focus on your own personal gain

Complete Activity # 6a & 6b
Relationship Builders & Relationship Breakers

Activity 6a: Relationship Builders & Relationship Breakers

Reflect on a time when you were the customer and the salesperson used a relationship 'builder' on you.

1

What was the selling situation?

What relationship builder was used?

How did this relationship builder make you feel?

What was the result of the situation? Did you buy from this salesperson and/or would you buy from this salesperson again?

Please turn over to complete activity.

Activity 6a: Continued

1 Reflect on a time when you were the customer and the salesperson used a relationship 'breaker' on you.

What was the selling situation?

_____

_____

_____

_____

What relationship breaker was used?

_____

_____

_____

_____

How did this relationship breaker make you feel?

_____

_____

_____

_____

What was the result of the situation? Did you buy from this salesperson and/or would you buy from this salesperson again?

_____

_____

_____

_____

_____

_____

_____

Now update your Learning Journal (page 59)

Activity 6b: Relationship Builders & Relationship Breakers

For each of the relationship 'breakers' listed below, explain how you could make this a relationship 'builder' ie, what could you do to make each of these negatives a positive in the sales process.

Relationship Breaker	How could you make this a Relationship Builder?
Wait for a problem to develop	
Focus only on making the sale	
Over-promise and under-deliver	
Wait for your customer to call	
Lie or make exaggerated claims	
Use the "us versus them" approach	
Blame somebody else	
Knock your competitors	
Focus on personal gain	

Now update your Learning Journal (page 59)

1

"You'll never have a product or price advantage again. They can be easily duplicated, but a strong customer service culture can't be copied."

Jerry Fritz

tpc ★

Top Ten Tips

Part 6 →

Top Ten Tips for Relationship Selling

Much of relationship selling is contained in the "non-selling' part of the sales process and is based on reputation, quality, ability to deliver, consistency and stability. Every time a customer problem is solved or a customer need is satisfied, the selling organization proves to the customer that their business makes sense.

This is relationship selling - the ongoing maintenance and nurturing of mutually beneficial business transactions that leads to further sales. Following are the top 10 tips for making Relationship Selling work.

"The quality of a person's life is determined more by their commitment to excellence than by any other factor, no matter what the external circumstances."

Vince Lombardi

 ## Be open and honest

A lot of business is referral business, and your communication needs to be reliable. If customer 'x' tells customer 'y' to use your services, then the story told to customer 'y' needs to be the same as the one that 'x' heard.

Be consistent

With referral and relationship-based selling, you are often not the first person telling your story. If you change your rates depending on who you are talking to, your referrals will ultimately stop. You need to be the same person to the small customers as you are to the big ones.

Listen

Listen, and then listen some more. Sales calls are all about active listening. Record and summarize what you hear, then repeat back to ensure that you have understood. Let the customer know what you will do for them, based on what you have heard.

4 Follow-up

Deliver accurately and on-time. Do what you say you are going to do, when you say you are going to do it. You are the 'guardian' of your customer and have a responsibility for what happens after the sale.

> "It starts with respect. If you respect the customer as a human being, and truly honor their right to be treated fairly and honestly, every thing else is much easier."
>
> Author Unknown

Take pride in what you have to sell

If you know your product well, and understand what your customer's needs, you will build relationships faster and close sales more efficiently. Take the time to really get to know your product and its suitability for your customers. Be enthusiastic about how you can work with your customer to solve their problems and meet their needs in the true spirit of partnership.

Know when not to sell and whom to refer a sale to

There are times when you will not be the right fit for a sale. Nothing is better than being able to tell a prospective customer that you aren't the right fit, and being able to recommend them to someone who is. That customer will call on you repeatedly if you continue to "do right" by them.

Care about your customers

Respect your customers' time. Always ask if they have time to meet or talk, and always be on time. If a customer has an urgent need then do everything possible to help them out. If you are genuine about what you want to do for your customer you will have them for a lifetime.

Never make a customer feel like "just a sale"

Remember that you are there first and foremost to help your customer with a solution to their problem, and secondly to add the customer to your quota list. At the same time, you are in business to make money. Explain to your customers your costs and fee structures so that they understand your business also. If asked to compromise value for cost, take the high road and let the customer know that you pride yourself on your values and won't compromise this for a sale.

 Stay focused

To be consistent, timely and reliable, you need to be organized and focused. Manage your time and allocate the right amount of time to making a sale so that you are able to be on time and not rushed.

10 Have fun!

If you don't have fun doing your job, you will sell less. Selling is not about pulling one over on someone. It's about problem-solving and working with a customer toward a solution. A customer needs something from you. You have a product or service that solves a problem for your customer. Remember it's a two-way street.

 Complete Activity # 7

Top Tips

Activity 7: Top Tips

1

Pick your top three tips and explain how you will use these to improve relationships with your customers.

Top Tip	I will implement this tip by...

Now update your Learning Journal (page 59)

Section 2

Learning Journal

The Learning Journal is used throughout the Learning Short-take™ process to record your key learnings, hot tips and things to remember.

Update your Learning Journal at anytime throughout the Learning Short-take™ process. Ensure you complete your Learning Journal after you finish each activity. Then turn back to the Participant Guide to continue your learning.

Learning Journal

As you work through this Learning Short-take™, make detailed notes on this page of the lessons you have learned and any useful skill areas. For each lesson or refresher point think about how you could further develop this skill. Your coach will want to discuss these with you in your Skill Development Action Planning meeting.

"…that is what learning is.
You suddenly understand something you've understood all your life, but in a new way."

Doris Lessing

"Anyone who stops learning is old, whether at twenty or eighty."

Henry Ford

"Act as though it were impossible to fail. "

Winston Churchill

"The wise do at once what the fool does later."
Baltasar Gracian (1601-58), Spanish Jesuit priest and author.

Learning or Idea	Action to be taken	Result Expected

2

Learning Journal - continued

Learning or Idea	Action to be taken	Result Expected

"Anyone who stops learning is old, whether at twenty or eighty."
Henry Ford

Learning or Idea	Action to be taken	Result Expected

"A customer is the most important visitor
on our premises, he is not dependent on us.
We are dependent on him.

He is not an interruption in our work.
He is the purpose of it.

He is not an outsider in our business.
He is part of it.

We are not doing him a favor by serving him.
He is doing us a favor by giving us an
opportunity to do so."

Mahatma Gandhi

Section 3

Skill Development
Action Plan

Your Skill Development Action Plan is the last Step in the Learning
Short-take™ process. After you have completed the Participant Guide
and all Activities update your Learning Journal then complete this section.

Skill Development Action Plan

This is the most important part of the program - your individual Skill Development Action Plan.

You need to complete this plan before meeting with your manager or prior to on-going coaching. You will discuss it in detail with your manager or coach as he or she will ensure that you have everything you need to complete the tasks and activities.

Once you have completed your **Skill Development Action Plan** schedule a meeting time with your manager or coach to review your plan. Take your participant guide and all other documentation received during the training course to this meeting.

Remember - you have committed to your **Skill Development Action Plan**, and need to make time to complete your tasks!

"The mind, once stretched by a new idea,
never regains its original dimensions."

Oliver Wendell Holmes

"Whatever you can do or dream you can - begin it.
Boldness has genius, power and magic."

Johann Wolfgang von Goethe

"Imagination is the eye of the soul."
Joseph Joubert (1754-1824)

Task or activity (Be specific)	Measure (this will help you to know you have achieved it)	Date (Be specific)
Reflect on your Learning Journal. Transfer action items that you can apply to your job. Ensure that you include some 'stretch goals' and also a blend of short, medium and long term goals.	Apart from you, who else is needed to assist you in achieving your goal.	Be specific. A general date such as 'Quarter 1', 'August', or 'by end of year' is vague and more likely to result in not achieving your target. Be specific – e.g. 22nd November.

3

Ideas for discussion with my manager

Ideas

Congratulations!

You've now completed this Learning Short-take™.

Meet with your Manager/Coach to discuss your
Skill Development Action Plan.

Suggested Reading

Tracy, Brian, 2003. Be a Sales Superstar: 21 Great Ways to Sell More, Faster, Easier in Tough Markets. Berrett-Koehler Publishers Inc.

Collis, Jack, 1998. When Your Customer Wins, You Can't Lose. Australia. Harper Collins.

Cathcart, Jim, 1990. Relationship Selling: The Key to Getting and Keeping Customers. Berklev Publishing Group.

"The only thing that matters is how you touch people. Have you given anyone insight? That's what I want to have done. Insight lasts; theories don't."

Peter Drucker

extra

Quick Reference

This Quick Reference provides you with a summary of key concepts, models and reference material from Learning Short-takes™. We have also included some quotations to ponder.

Use this section as a quick reference to keep your learning active.

4

“ 85 percent of the happiness and success you enjoy in life will be determined by the quality of relationships with others. ”

Brian Tracy

Relationship Selling

In selling there is one simple truth - most of the business you do is based on the relationships that you have with your customers, and your best customers are the ones with whom you have the best relationships. Relationship selling is simple. If you want your customers to come back they have to like you, respect you and trust you.

4

" **Your professionalism is defined not by the business you are in, but by the way you are in business.** "

Tony Alessandra

Evolution of the Selling Function

4

1. Pure Transaction: Basic early selling – standard commodity products, price and reliability – there is little to build on, business may be spasmodic, hand-to-mouth and unpredictable.

2. Relationship and Trust: Continuity, consistency, sustainability, and some understanding of the customer's real issues are seen to have value by both selling and buying organization; intangibles begin to be regarded as relevant benefits.

4. Partnership: Activities of the buying and selling organization become almost seamless; the supplier is virtually part of the customer's organization and treated as such; there is a level of anticipation, innovation and integrated support that is very difficult to un-pick, even if it were in the customer's interests to do so. This is the pinnacle of relationship selling.

3. Management and Information: A longer-term supply arrangement is seen as an advantage by seller and buyer, because it brings extra intangible benefits of co-operation and support other areas of the customer's business – improving the customer's own competitive strengths and operating efficiencies.

4

" Do a little bit more than average and from that point on your progress multiplies itself out of all proportion to the effort put in. "

Paul J. Meyer

The Changing Face of Selling

Traditional Selling	Modern Selling
standard product	customized, flexible, tailored product and service
seller has product knowledge	seller has strategic knowledge of customer's market-place and knows all implications and opportunities resulting from product/service supply relating to customer's market-place
value is represented and judged according to selling price	value is assessed according to the cost to the customer, plus non-financial implications with respect to CSR (corporate social responsibility), environment, ethics, and corporate culture
benefits of supply extend to products and services only	benefits of supply extend way beyond products and services, to relationship, continuity, and any assistance that the selling organization can provide to the customer
seller knows the customers needs	seller knows the needs of the customers' customers, partners and suppliers
strategic emphasis is on new business growth (ie, acquiring new customers)	strategic emphasis is on customer retention and increasing business to those customers (although new business is still sought)

4

" Customers do not buy products. They buy solutions to a problem. "

Jack Collis

Inside the Sales Call

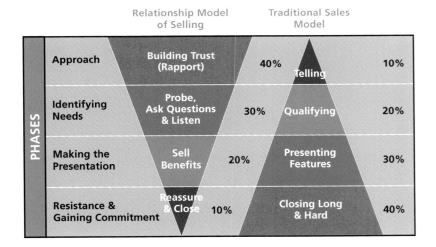

PHASES	Relationship Model of Selling			Traditional Sales Model	
Approach	Building Trust (Rapport)	40%	Telling		10%
Identifying Needs	Probe, Ask Questions & Listen	30%	Qualifying		20%
Making the Presentation	Sell Benefits	20%	Presenting Features		30%
Resistance & Gaining Commitment	Reassure & Close	10%	Closing Long & Hard		40%

4

❝ Honesty is the first chapter of the book of wisdom. ❞

Thomas Jefferson

Relationship Builders & Relationship Breakers

Relationship Builders	Relationship Breakers
■ Treat customers like life-long partners	■ Waiting for a problem to develop
■ Become a solutions provider	■ Focusing only on making the sale
■ Deliver more service than you promise	■ Over-promise and under-deliver
■ Schedule regular service calls	■ Wait for your customers to call you
■ Develop open and honest communication	■ Lie or make exaggerated claims
■ Use the 'we can' approach	■ Use the "us versus them" approach
■ Take responsibility for mistakes made	■ Blame somebody else
■ Be an ally for the customers' business	■ Knock a competitor
	■ Focus on your own personal gain

4

" The quality of a person's life is determined more by their commitment to excellence than by any other factor, no matter what the external circumstances. "

Vince Lombardi

Top Ten Tips for Relationship Selling

4

1. Be open and honest

2. Be Consistent

3. Listen

4. Follow-Up

5. Take Pride in what you have to sell

6. Know when not to sell and whom to refer a sale to

7. Care about your customers

8. Never make a customer feel like just a sale

9. Stay focused

10. Have fun!

4

" The very best salespeople are 'relationship experts'. They focus all of their attention on the relationship before they begin talking about their products or services. "

Brian Tracy

Next Steps

Congratulations! You have now completed this Learning Short-take™ title. The entire list of Learning Short-takes™ can be found on the TPC website.

In this section we have suggested Learning Short-take™ titles for you that will build your learning. You may order these Learning Short-takes™ online at **www.tpc.net.au**

Customer Service Excellence
Delighting Your Customers and Your Manager

Learning Short-take™ Outline

The people we need to build our business are out there. They are waiting to experience the good feelings that go with having their expectations met. They are constantly searching for satisfaction and recognition of their worth as customers. The great opportunity awaiting every business today is the chance to give excellent customer service that results in the customer coming back again and again.

This Learning Short-take™ combines self-study with workplace activities to facilitate customer service excellence. Participants will evaluate their current approach to customer service and develop new horizons to become a true customer service professional.

This Learning Short-take™ is designed for completion in approximately 90 minutes.

Learning Objectives

- Define the skills and attributes of an effective customer service professional.

- Explain the Customer Satisfaction Model.

- Identify Customer Types and Customer Needs.

- Implement strategies to retain dissatisfied customers.

- Explain the 5-Step Customer Service Model.

- Use superior communication skills to enhance customer interactions.

Course Content

- Part 1: Customer Service Self Assessment - Assessment of current skills and creation of Customer Service Profile

- Part 2: Identifying the skills and attributes of an effective customer service professional

- Part 3: The Results Model

- Part 4: Customer Types and Customer Needs

- Part 5: The Customer Satisfaction Model

- Part 6: Customer Service Communication Skills

- Part 7: Calming Upset Customers

- Part 8: The 5-Step Customer Service Model

Influencing for Opportunity
Identify and Maximize Ways to Influence

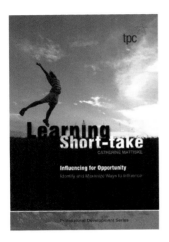

Course Content

- Part 1: Fundamentals of Influence

- Part 2: Influence: A Choice

- Part 3: Naturally Occurring Influence Patterns

- Part 4: Methods of Persuasion

- Part 5: The Challenges of Influence

- Part 6: Building a life of Influence

Learning Short-take™ Outline

The ability to Influence others is critical in today's competitive business environment. Organizations run on influence. Influence enables you to build the relationships you need to get results inside or outside the formal power structure. In order for people to succeed in the flattened hierarchy of the modern corporate environment, they must be able to influence others. Employees and managers alike can no longer assume they have power over others - they must earn it through influence. However we are not born as influential people. This is a skill which must be learned and practiced.

This Learning Short-take™ combines self-study with workplace activities to provide you with the key skills and techniques to influence those around you. You will learn models of influence, influence principles and strategies, as well as how to plan and prepare for important influence opportunities. As a result of this Learning Short-take™ you will achieve greater results in your organization, work more productively and effectively in a team environment, and develop stronger working relationships with co-workers, suppliers, customers, and even competitors.

The Learning Short-take™ is designed for completion in approximately 90 minutes.

Learning Objectives

- Identify patterns of influence.

- Evaluate how you currently use influence behaviors and identify areas for development.

- Develop influence behaviors for greater personal and business success.

- Establish clear and powerful influence goals.

- Increase influence to overcome resistance.

- Describe how to ask for and receive support.

- Design an approach for formal and informal influence situations; apply the approach to a real-life situation.

- Create a Skill Development Action Plan.

Understanding Customer Motivation
Get Inside the Customer's Mind

Learning Short-take™ Outline

Customers are interested in products and services that fulfil their needs and wants. If a customer doesn't have a perceived need or want then it is unlikely that they will buy. As an experienced salesperson, you must create need and motivate your customers to want to own or use the products and services that you sell.

This Learning Short-take™ combines self-study with workplace activities to help you understand the elements of customer motivation. You will develop tips, tricks and techniques to encourage your customers to start or continue to do business with you, and get the products and services that they need.

This Learning Short-take™ is designed for completion in approximately 90 minutes.

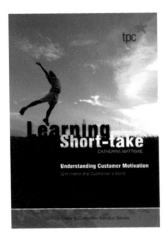

Learning Objectives

- Explain the psychology of buying and the elements of customer motivation.
- Explain the importance of creating value for customers and the impact on customer motivation.
- Identify value opportunities in your business.
- Explain why customers buy and the impact of buying objectives and buying influences.
- Develop strategies for aligning customer behavior types with need creation opportunities.
- Create a Skill Development Action Plan.

Course Content

- Part 1: Understanding ROI
- Part 2: Measurement Myths
- Part 3: Kirkpatrick's Model
- Part 4: Measuring through Review
- Part 5: Bringing it Together

5

TPC - The Performance Company is known world wide as 'the place to go' for Corporate Training Courses, Train the Trainer and Instructional Design Programs.

Corporate Training Division

> Global Learning Platform - Coordinate your training worldwide
> Instructional Design - Customized courses for your organization
> Trainer Development - Maximize your training effectiveness
> Coaching - Get the best from your participants
> Strategic Consulting - Helping clients meet their goals

Learning Short-takes™ Division

> Professional Development
> Sales and Customer Service
> Leadership and Management
> Trainer Development
> Able to be customized for individual clients

www.tpc.net.au

New York • California • Sydney • London